Advanced I
AT THE BEGINNIN(

C000242082

"This poetry collection is absolutel͵   ͝   ͺ
gant, thought-worthy, and lyrical. A must-read, for sure."
~ Flor Ana, Author of *A Moth Fell In Love With The Moon*

"Visual, cryptic, and beautiful poetry, *At The Beginning Of Yesterday* has it all and everything in between. The reader is able to drift off into a world of mindfulness as each poem causes the reader to think. Reading the words of Tiffiny Rose Allen is easy, exciting, and meaningful."
~ Amelie Honeysuckle, Author of *What Once Was An Inside Out Rainbow*

"With every poem, I felt a release of my breath and an ease of connection. These poems were simply stunning, melodic, and human. This book is a true treasure to my shelf and heart."
~ Kendall Hope, Author of *Pockets of Lavender*

"*At The Beginning of Yesterday* is a beautiful compilation of poetry that takes you on a journey of hope and forgiveness of the self that comes around full circle. The imagery and metaphors used by Allen ground you to the world and the universal moments we share. I am looking for the roots growing beside me. Thank you, Tiffiny."
~ Erin Flanagan, Author of *Haikus to Irish Tunes*

"Weaving femininity, the mystical, and evocative images in nature, Allen's work is not only ethereal, but empowering. It's the perfect book to gift your mother or your girlfriends."
~ Annie Vazquez, Founder of The Fashion Poet

Edited by Flor Ana Mireles

1st Edition | 01

Paperback ISBN: 979-8-9869891-6-7

First Published February 2023

For inquiries and bulk orders, please email:
indieearthpublishinghouse@gmail.com

Also Available In
Hardback:
979-8-9869891-8-1

Ebook:
979-8-9869891-7-4

Indie Earth Publishing Inc.
| Miami, FL |

INDIE EARTH
PUBLISHING

AT THE BEGINNING OF YESTERDAY

Tiffiny Rose Allen

Other works by Tiffiny Rose Allen

Leave The Dreaming To The Flowers (2017)

Tell The Monster Who You Are (2018)

A Rainbow Against A Darkened Sky (2019)

Canorous:
Words Written In The Age Of Social Distancing (2020)

The Parables Of A Hopeful Life Seeker:
Or Just Another Collection Of Shadow Work (2020)

We Are Based Off Our Dreamscapes (2021)

Leave The Dreaming To The Flowers:
5 Year Anniversary Revised Edition (2022)

Dreams In Hiding:
an amalgamation of verses and prose (Curated 2022)

For the ones who hope for a better tomorrow

"Yesterday I was clever, so I wanted to change the world. Today I am wise, so I am changing myself."

~ Rumi

INTRODUCTION

Yesterday is sometimes seen as a long time ago. It feels like just yesterday that I was a little kid, without too much of a careful thought. Seems the same as when I went grocery shopping then came home and watched a movie. Time is quite illusory and strange. What we looked at from before seems either farther away or closer. We are either selfish or unselfish; we simplify or we elaborate. The formation and the passages all blend and form together to make a big mess of what we call a lifetime of plentitudes.

This collection of poetry is my farewell letter to a past version of myself. A version that was so far away and so near at the same time. I've gone through and I've processed, I've recycled and I've changed, in some odd way. I've become a little more selfish with my time and my actions, and I've prioritized putting myself first and not caring so much about what other people think, and I am grateful to have reached this point, but I would not be here without the past. I might make many more mistakes and I might do and say the wrong thing from time to time, but I am happy to be here nonetheless.

It has been a grand journey to step into myself, and I am grateful for the time that allowed me to process how far I have come. I am bound by mortality to continue to journey and grow, and along the way, I'll keep sharing a few words or so.

I hope that, in your becoming, you show yourself some compassion. I hope you know that you are not a terrible person for wanting more for yourself. I hope you know that it is quite alright to grieve things that you no longer desire, and it is even better to fall in love with life in ways you had given up on or not expected. It is alright to be a little selfish and it is alright to pick yourself up and take a chance at something new. Yesterday might be right behind you, or even farther still, and it will be alright, no matter which way. It will be alright because you're not in the past anymore. You're right here, with a tomorrow peeking over the trees, and pushing through the clouds.

Signed,

Tiffiny Rose Allen

Sometimes I feel just like I did years ago,
suffocating under the bitter guise of
what others consider love to be.

I ransomed spirits to guide you back to me
and I don't know if I could do it again. See,

it's not up to me to be strong. It's up to you now.

Are you ready for this phase?
Can you trust yourself enough to love, to forgive yourself?

If love were to be a garden,
I would want the roots growing firmly beside me.

A Small And Lovely Flower

I forged my steps,
I walked over the cracks,
the sun was going down.
I didn't know how to digest
the day.

The small wonders,
the ponders of living and dreaming.

I spoke to the passerby, I didn't know their name.
They told me a story that brought tears to my eyes.

It was about a small and lovely flower,
blooming against the reality of time,
in between us,
in between us all.

Separate and perpetrate,
we are always wearing thin.
Our daily lives don't make us happy,
so we hide within.
I'm slipping through my own fingers.
I'm trying not to bruise my ego.

Maybe in the fairytales they always got it right,
but I never once saw a large castle in my sight.

TIFFINY ROSE ALLEN

I was quite alright with my cottage and my sun,
wouldn't give up my truth for a momentary splendor.
I was quite alright with what you said to me.
You didn't want the cake or any of the coffee.

It was just okay because I said I'd love you anyway.
Small flower,
small flower,

maybe all your petals bloomed because they deemed it fit.
Maybe the wind blew through my hair and opened it to see
through veils of uncertainty, seeing what will be.

I woke from my dream, I didn't know its name.
It told me a story about a small and lovely flower.

It told me the days of when I was to know...

The flowers bloom just like joy
and it is known as peace.

AT THE BEGINNING OF YESTERDAY

Pocket Watch

Waiting for the clock to turn,
my pocket watch keeps stopping.

I'm winding the gears,
letting things go.

Don't break the spinner,
don't break the fold.

Just flow.
It moves
forward and backward
upon its chain,

tethered through the belt loops and
tick tick tick.

The hands move on and on
as an adventure brews,
turning into a grand entrance

the green from the brush whispering secrets,
the concrete pavement on galaxies of different ideals.

Car wheels,
exhaust, steering wheel,

turning corners and singing to the sky
a daily lullaby.

Perhaps it's true that time doesn't really mean anything.
Maybe it's just something we say as a way
to make it seem like more of an ordeal.

Cold Pillowcases

My day was beautiful today.
I worked hard and I laughed, oh how I laughed with a dear friend.
Smiles that couldn't help themselves and eyes that sparkled with
amusement.

Then, I came back to my bed at the end of the day and all the smiles
fell to decay.

My mind filled up with all the things the sunlight permitted me to
ignore.
The moon drew back the curtain and
Now my mind goes, goes, goes...

Goes to that burdened place,
where the demons crawl and the 'what ifs' poke and prod.

I wonder what you're doing and I wonder if you think of me and
I wonder what would happen if I took a chance and changed that
theme and got a new job and told you I loved you and said farewell
and traveled the world and took out loans I couldn't afford and said
'oh well' to everything I had ever ignored...

And I wonder why I don't do those things and I wonder why I feel so
stuck and I wonder why the nighttime makes my mind spin as it does.

I wonder why I seem to not be good enough and why they always leave. Taking my trust and crushing it, crushing it, crushing it. I loved you more than any, I loved you more than I knew how to.

I wonder where the love I had for myself has gone to. Right now, all I can do is lay my head down on cold pillowcases.

Hollow.

The Same Song

Winter wanders in.
Heaters get turned up.
The snow we've all been preparing for
begins to fall.

I'll play the same song again and again,
waiting for the next conversation.

I have no idea what this means except for everything.

Just Like Them

Magnitude of fair retrogrades,
you sit there and you change the pace.
I marveled at dresses of lace.
I prayed to be just like them.

Tired eyes,
sullen face.
We keep moving on ,
singing our prayerful songs of grandeur.
Sitting impatiently,
waiting patiently,

contradicting our remarks,
but we keep steady.

Karma Cigarettes

Wash away all your karma with some smoke.
Figure out where your incense or your cigarette can rest.

Take a deep breath
or tense up.
It's your choice,
however you wish to rack up the points.

The spirits watch you now as
you dangle your hands by your sides.

The karma cigarettes are burning out.
Your overthinking wrapped up in
turmoils of ashen ideas.

Figuring out which move to make,
which path to tread,
as the coins keep racking up for your
karmic fate.

Which move do you wish to make?

As The Sunset

Carved out of sugar,
carved out of gain.

Coffee warmed up touches my lips.
I lean in to take a sip and
it turns cold.

Winter's calmed down.
I'm working on changing my frown.

I opened the door,
I stepped out and I saw it ...

Lavender dreams are forming
purples and blues. I saw sunsets gleaming with views.
You know they know that they are beautiful.

I passed out my name like candy,
sugar and sweet and lingering,

trying my best to be persistent and allow the morning to reveal the
day's plan.
Should I take it by the reins?

Maybe I won't know, maybe I won't be as the sunset
unless I try to be.

AT THE BEGINNING OF YESTERDAY

The colors are beautiful in the morning
and the clouds too.

TIFFINY ROSE ALLEN

Today's Society

Kindness seems a luxury.
Everyone seems to always be out to get the other.

Hang on.

"How can I benefit from this?
Does it inconvenience the both of us or only you? Just you?
Okay, that's fine, let me turn my eyes back to my sunrise.
I don't mind if you despise.
I want to sip on my money
and laugh at your dismay,
running around,
trying to keep your head above the water.
What a pity we're born this way.
If only my hand could reach out
and help you..."
says the rich man to the poor.

So, we build up our homes brick by brick.
Constantly being told to pick ourselves up and
get over it.

AT THE BEGINNING OF YESTERDAY

New Sidewalks

A trial, an error, a dance, a despair.
An absolutely everything and a sudden no.
I turn around and I'm thrown back into the show.

Same song on repeat, on repeat, on repeat.
Retrograde is certainly taking its toll on me.
But,
I'm still showing up.

That was the number—222.

New sidewalks crumble as I turn onto them
and the only person I ever want to talk to is you.

They must have played a cruel joke on me,
dangling in front of my eyes "happiness, here you go,"
but it wasn't. And it doesn't.
So much more to life than reeling over these thoughts.
Yet, I'm fine.
I'm really fine.
I'm just, you know,
really missing my best friend tonight.

Stuck on the wonder of the path that was previewed then rushed away,
yet held fast forward buttons and eternity all at once.
A beautiful paradox of things I've come to cherish, one could say.

TIFFINY ROSE ALLEN

Time was held within a separate chapter not so long ago,
then transformed to turn around again.
What a wild reality of chaos and love.

Friends and Enemies

They say keep your friends close and your enemies closer.
What's a friend but a foe you've saved for later?
Here I am,
digging into my demons.
A souvenir.
They say you learn
and you always get to keep them.

A closet keepsake.
Hang it up to dry amongst your sweaters.
Unpack it for later.
Unpack it.
Unpack it.

Don't keep it there.

What's a friend but someone you can depend on?
What's a friend but someone you've shared a laugh with?
What's a friend but someone who'll always be there?
What's a friend but someone who won't run when you get scared?

A toss of a coin.
A gamble for luck.
A choice we make.
Meeting people.
Simple word exchanges

decide our current fates,
stepping forward parallel.

Starts off by saying "Hi."

Entertainment

I miss the red velvet curtains.

My movie trailer of symphonies.
The stringed quartet playing another melody.

Look at all the pretty pictures.
I'm scrubbing the dishes,
doing what I can to

rest assured

I tried taking care of everything,
but I must
hold space
for myself
first.

My soul has been drained.
I need to restrain and no longer
be
the entertainment.

TIFFINY ROSE ALLEN

Just Like That

Just like that,
snap of the fingers.

A merry go round,
just as soon as it's opened, it's ended.

Party favors passed around,
traveling, going to and going fro,

not realizing the cost of the splendor.
Just changing the mood,
a semi-permanent fixture,
it came and it went
and the lesson was fluid.

How time changes everything, how time changes nothing, how street
lights go out and how minds fill with doubt.

The ending, beginning, mind is made up.
I'm losing, I'm winning.
The merry-go-round keeps on spinning.

We tried our best, I guess.

Cycles Shifting

Clothespinned curtains,
hanging onto strings like
feathered wings.

Wind keeps blowing,
beckoning,
waiting for the fabric to
dry.

A sound
touched
spiral
makes the colors go up like rainbow dust
in the forest
where the mundane ran back home to sit.

Sewing Needle

You see,
I turned my rage into art.
My heart had finished bleeding so there was nothing left but to stitch
up the wound.

My sewing needle of fate forming a repetition,
a clandestine healing.

It Flickers As I Dance

The light comes and goes.
It flickers as I dance around the room,
The moonbeams slide under me as I tiptoe through the walls.
My own beloved place to be.

I climb the empty stairs.
They creak, they chatter,
telling me the secrets of all the places I plan to see.

Where will you be, where will the sun rise from, in the morn—
I mourn, still.

You know the feeling of the daffodils,
the fields all full in bloom.

I'll yield soon when I see the yellow
matching the patchwork of my gown,
the frilly one.

The one that makes me forget that I have to-do lists and reasonings
for thinking we're so immortal in a passing portal of a world.

Dear, you must stop making yourself so small.
You must shine that light just like you've known.

TIFFINY ROSE ALLEN

You've seen it before, you can remember it still.
It'll help, you'll see, it will.

25

UNIVERSAL SECRETS PRINTED OUT IN NEWSPAPERS

22 February 2023   **A Poem**

I often feel like my anxiety
inconveniences other people more than
it inconveniences me. Like my reaction
to a situation is worse than me handling
the feelings that arise within me.
Maybe it is a mixture of both, who
knows?
I travel miles just to come home to
myself, and I'm glad that I have me—I
embrace my beloved new beginning and
I do my best to set everything else free,
yet still there resides anxiety.

I think—
Was I loyal to myself this year?
Did I love as much as I could; was I a
dumb fool for doing so?
Did I ever open up again?

What am I to do but continue on like
there is
no sticky glue stopping me from being
how I want to be?
The fear will always surface, I know, the
overthinking and the mess,
but so will hope and love and joy, too.

What I did and didn't do
to hang on or let go of you...you;
the past version of myself,
the mark of plenty and enough and of
change.

Why are you so worried about taking up
the space of being wanted?
I sit around and criticize myself and get
choked up about it later

when all I really need to do is get myself
to snap out of it; but
how do you snap out of it when it's
yourself telling you you're worn?

My poetry, my anxiety, my propriety,

I guess I must push through it, right? I
don't know how else to handle it other
than to ground myself and know that I
am on the path of what I know to be
right for me, and for a few moments
here and there, when the imposter
syndrome recedes, I find that I am
happy, and that there is worth in the
perseverance.

At the end of the day, I sometimes find
myself thinking of yesterday
and I find that I truly believe that people
create art because they have to,
not so much because they want to
or perhaps one slightly outweighs the
other, but
I don't think I have ever created
something simply because I wanted to.

It was either out of heartache,
heartbreak, spite, or those precious
moments of love and joy.

With every word I stitch, I tie them up
with laces of hope because
I don't want to know what the world is
like
I don't want to know what I am like
without it.

If ever I'm to forget my hope,
I write down barrels and barrels of
words so that they can remind me

that hope is never gone for long;
it just needs to get some air from time to
time.

The circles I pace around in dissipate
and I find myself walking through fields
of moss on cold-dew mornings.

The sun peeking up, offering some
encouragement,
letting me know that I am alright
where I am,
I am alright with the thought of
yesterday
and letting it be what it has been.

The spinning cycle of a galaxy telling us
all the secrets of astrology,
universal secrets printed out in
newspapers:

*You might be prone to
overthinking today—
don't let it get you
down!*

Tiffiny Rose Allen

It Was Significant

What a radical night shift.
Feels like a magnificence.
Finding different curtains, different themes,
different elemental beams.

Making blue look like the sun,
making them feel like they're the one.

Secondary is not the aim,

because it was significant,
like a signature lipstick.
Paint red upon my lips,
kiss my fingers, kiss my hips

Gazing mirrors.
Peering souls.

Letting go of the controls.
Shadowed eyelids blink the message
of the morning
we've got to keep on turning.

TIFFINY ROSE ALLEN

Colors Forming As Band-Aids Come Sundown

To be stitched together is to have bled.
I dipped my flower petals in the waters of magnificence.
I drank the drops that fell
so simply,
my eyes opening to find that...

To be happy is not to hold.
To be peaceful is not to be perfect.
To be anything other than what we are is
not to change overnight.
As boats to a lighthouse,
a bruised heart seeks to heal.

We take the beauty of the sunset and
apply it to our souls,
for
to be stitched together is to have bled,
colors forming as band-aids come sundown.

AT THE BEGINNING OF YESTERDAY

Perspectives of a Looking Glass

Gazing at the moving world,
can I, too, move as you?

Can I whisper in the locks with keys and
open every door?

Or should I answer the telephone as it rings,
open a window for the birdsong?

Should I exit every greeting with a fair and fond *Hello*?
Maybe I am to paint the seams with the light reflected off of me
as the sun goes down and hides behind the darkened drapes,
a mere rainbow's greeting for a while.

I move just as you do throughout the day.
I've studied you more than anyone.

The way you move your hair behind your ear,
the way you check your eyes and fix your coat,
the way you take just a moment to admire yourself and
the way you check your hair when company is around.

I've studied you, I've seen you, so up close, so personal, so provocative
and conservative. I've seen you in your glory and I've seen you at your
worst. I've seen you age and grow and throw the flower pots out of
rage...

TIFFINY ROSE ALLEN

I've seen you pick up each and every shard of me,
as I lay upon the ground.
I've seen you gasp as you place your finger to your lips.
My last bite

as I gave you nothing but the love of me, my time of day, my time
capsule.

My reflection was always you, and you come back and place another
me where you had once placed me before.

AT THE BEGINNING OF YESTERDAY

On The Other Side

I feel like I'm on the other side of the mirror.
A parallel escape.
A continuous structure, but different, so very different.

Greener and brighter over here,
I can catch my breath and not sink
into my mind

as I have done before.

I feel like I'm on the other side of the mirror.
I have my own garden now.
I have my delicate petals of persistence
that carried me through.

A drop of rain as I hesitate, a tap upon
reflections as we see that it really was just all the same.

It is different now.

I hang up the adornments as I make my way through the house and I
catch a glimpse of myself here and there and I see,

I see someone who is still figuring it out, but holds contentment
closer to them now.

TIFFINY ROSE ALLEN

Roses With Wire-Wrapped Belonging

I have my sweater on,
the one with all the roses spread upon it.

I saw patches of gold in the stars last night.

It was lovely.
It was iridescent.

Reminded me of so much love and belonging.

The shooting stars,

I wire-wrapped them and
hung them 'round my neck.

I glanced and saw a new light shining.
A constellation of different charts
pointing towards the way.

The moon travels down and invites in the sun rays.

Midnight was shining when I looked at the city
so full and so pretty.

I have my sweater on,
the one with all the roses spread upon it.

AT THE BEGINNING OF YESTERDAY

I'd like to have a garden box
so that I could plant some leaves and maybe when they're grown,

I'll be able to go and pluck them and make us both some tea.
I see a garden growing with someone.
I see a garden growing,
just like the sprouting roses upon my sweater.

Sea Glass

Do not be discouraged if your anger consumes you suddenly.
Do not be discouraged for your expression showing forth.
You see,
we are the Earth and
just as the sky rains and thunders,
just as the oceans roar,
our emotions are allowed
to flow.

To be that calm and resolved stereotypical spiritual highlight of a
personality
is to void out the human experience.

To be spiritual, we must flow and
to flow is to go through the emotions.

As the sea accepts glass bottles tossed over from ships,
it shapes and polishes and molds the pieces according to their journey.

And just as the other shells and stones are tumbled and
ushered to the shoreline,
the glass is accepted amongst the lot and
acknowledged as part of the sea.

Let your tears fall, dear.
You're not forsaken
for feeling.

Rock Polish

Maybe if I was just a little more polished—
not a modern rock and not an old one,
somewhere in the middle—
maybe I'd be found,
picked from the stream,
gently molded and sanded down by the water that surrounded me.
Maybe I'd be just a little jagged
and just a little smoother than I am now.
Maybe my poetry would reach your ears.
Maybe you'd find some hope again.
Maybe somehow maybe
I don't remember the saying
and I won't rush the polish.
I've got to let the water hold me just a little bit more.

Moths

It would seem that everywhere I go, I see moths. And I don't know why.

I keep having dreams that I'm walking around the streets of somewhere else.
I keep seeing moths at every corner that I turn.
I keep sensing that it is always yesterday
and somehow I am *here*.

It's interesting because moths don't make me think about you. But whenever I remember that moths don't make me think about you, it makes me think about you. And it's funny how that works, right? Because, in realizing that I'm not thinking about you, it makes me think about you. And it seems like everywhere I look, and everywhere I go, I see the numbers that I would see whenever I was with you. I see the address of that building where I met you for the first time, whenever you stepped off that fucking bus. And, sometimes, I wonder what would have happened if you wouldn't have stepped off that bus and if you wouldn't have gotten on the bus in the first place. And I think, *What would have happened?* And then, I also think that I still would have felt very small and I still would have felt very caged and I still would have felt very inadequate, and I still feel so inadequate, but it's in a very different way now. It's in a very different way now.
And I know that I've grown, and I know that I've gotten better... And now, it seems everywhere I look I see moths, and so many people see moths as negative or bad or horrible. And I... Well, I'm not really sure

what I see moths as, but I know that they are drawn to the light. And it doesn't matter if it is a flame. Or if it is a lamp. If it is natural or artificial. The moth will always go towards the light. The moth will always take the chance of finding something beautiful.

Moths mean change, and they mean transformation. And they mean something different and something new, and maybe it's a new beginning. I've been trying so hard to work on a new beginning, something that will flow smoothly and well. I want it to go well.

But still, it would seem, everywhere I go, I see moths.

Autumn Nostalgia

They say that autumn is set aside for nostalgia.

But I have found that, this time, it has been set forward,

placed excitedly into the futurism of no longer holding, no longer hoping—

but drifting—
along the mist of
allowing.

I find myself going back and forth.
I'm so hardcore one moment, and then, I change my mind.

I go back and I go forward.

Each time I'm trying,
I'm trying.
I look and that's all I can do is try,
for if I don't,
I won't
be half as much as I could be.

And in the year that felt like many
all wrapped up into one,
the autumn changed my entire life around,

AT THE BEGINNING OF YESTERDAY

the betterment of my soul
residing
in a flow state.

TIFFINY ROSE ALLEN

A Feeling I Thought Would Never Quite Return

Even so, the clock runs out as I run to type this page, but

I don't fret or worry
as the new day begins.

I soften and I sway as my heart opens again.
A feeling I thought would never quite return,

until I saw the rain and I loved it like the sun.

I open up the curtains to peer into the sky
and so,
a song begins again.

AT THE BEGINNING OF YESTERDAY

Hi, Friend

I see you there.
You're just like me, I think.
I know how lonely you feel,
how judged and downtrodden it all seems.

It will get better, you know.
The wind ushers in a glorious change, something of beauty, something
of grandeur, something of ellipses and whispers.

An unknown circumstance, perhaps, but one that promises something
to remember; and I'll bet a good thing at that.

You have so much more that needs to be learned, but that doesn't mean
you shouldn't share what you already know.

That's how we grow, after all.

Imposter syndrome likes to hang out so that we might stay small be-
cause we often fear what is unknown.

But when we do face the things that scare us, it always seems like it was
kind of silly to be scared at all.

I don't think it demeans what we felt before. I just think that we don't
really stay the same, we keep growing.

We keep growing like how the earth grows, and moves, and flows.

The roots become intertwined with the blossoms of what yesterday had ushered in.

Inspiration Formed From Flower Petals

I think you can bloom and blossom just like anyone.
I think you can be brave if you really wanted to.
You can reach out to the sky and stand up tall just like the flowers
do—

Even when they waver,
they keep themselves held high,
opening themselves up for a little bit of sunshine.

Even when the rain falls,
you won't see them falling too
as inspiration is formed from flower petals.

TIFFINY ROSE ALLEN

Reading Over Tea

The teacups had crystals resting next to them.

A tonic for pursuing daydreams and keeping one on the ground.

The cards invoked Temperance,
a Saggitarian memorandum, the opposite of a Gemini,
the other side of the wheel,
Wheel of Fortune is pulled now.

A balance beckoned, an identifier,
a teacup spilling what is needed,
an herbal remedy, a melody, a dampened tablecloth of secrets.

Wring it out.
The Lovers is now pulled.

Balance has been restored.

45

AT THE BEGINNING OF YESTERDAY

My Evening Primrose

My evening primrose blossoms under the moon.
I enter the garden knowing that I'll see you soon.

I walk down by the stream and, in my eye, it gleams.
My evening primrose blooms,
and then, the bindweed, too,
moonbow and morning glory, moonglow

Tell me all that you know.

And when the moths are drawn to the wildflowers, I'll be with you.

46

TIFFINY ROSE ALLEN

Wishin' Me Luck

Flying over the sea with the moon and Jupiter right next to me.
Right there, wishin' me luck,
wishin' me luck.

Moths II

I don't see moths quite as much anymore. I still take note of them, but I don't see them quite as much as I used to. And now, when I see moths, I don't think of you; I think of me, and everything that I've been working towards. I think that maybe they are my new good luck charm and maybe I'm not doing things as badly as I so often think I am. Maybe things end and transition to different things so that we can see what we really needed the entire time. It was good for the growth, but sometimes, roots are not firmly in the soil, and sometimes, weeding our gardens opens up room for the new roots to take. Maybe 222 can mean I've found my way and maybe the moths wings can tell me that everything's okay.

Perhaps we can take comfort in the moth and its way of living, continuing to go about and thrive, regardless of the world's views around it. Is it dark, is it sad, is it something bad? Maybe a moth can just be a moth sometimes, and maybe I can be myself without worry.

At The Beginning Of Yesterday

At the beginning of yesterday,
I loved you.

For to love was freeing so much more than my own choice.

To love was unraveling everything I had resisted and been afraid of.

Loving was beautiful and it was everything it needed to be.

That sunrise,

at the beginning of yesterday,
Seemed to hold its hearts together.

Rightly so.

I waved at the trees as they began to rustle and sing,

and I think, what if we really are just stardust

spinning a web of magical uncertainty and fascinated glances through
telescopes and illusions of worlds and ideas set before us,

painting pictures with golden dewdrops of diligence and grandeur.

sophisticated anomalies and eyes staring straight into the same soul,

49

a union of fascination and peace.

A marking of a time that was profound and needed more than most.

The simplicity of a meadow,

blooming with daisies and pink wildflowers

while the wind tickled their petals and laughed, *"Hello, my darlings."*

At the beginning of yesterday, it was ever lovely, and beloved.

AT THE BEGINNING OF YESTERDAY

Now, I have come back to myself.

Now, I am showing that same everlasting love to myself.

My cares ran so deep I had forgotten how much love I truly needed,
too.

Roots will grow firmly beside me.

As I open my heart, discarding the shell that cracked open
so forcefully,

roots will grow.

A garden grows within the heart now.

It is time to turn the page,
thanking yesterday and
looking unto tomorrow.

Fin

Acknowledgments

As my first book publication with an independent press,
I am beyond grateful and feel incredibly blessed to have found the
perfect home for my little poetry collection.

I would like to thank my editor, Flor Ana Mireles, and
publisher, Indie Earth Publishing, for being so kind and
understanding throughout this entire process.
Thank you for hearing out all of my ideas and helping me shape
this book into what you are holding in your hands now.
I could not have asked for a better
experience for this collection.

I would also like to thank my friends, loved ones and
my family, for their support and encouragement throughout
this process. I would name each and every one of you,
but you all know who you are, and I hope you all know
how grateful I am for each of you. You are all loved endlessly.

*Thank you to every reader, dreamer, and creator,
not just for reading my own words, but for sharing yours as well.
Your art will always be needed.*

About The Author

Tiffiny Rose Allen is a writer, creator, and poet originally from the state of Florida. She began writing at an early age and self-published her first collection of poetry, *Leave The Dreaming To The Flowers*, in 2017. Her poetry is eclectic in portraying her views of the different aspects of life. When she is not somewhere writing, she is either creating something with her hands or working on anything and everything that excites her. Her work has been featured in numerous magazine and anthology publications, including *The Elpis Pages*, *The Feminine Macabre*, and *Dreamer by Night Magazine*. In 2022, she curated her very own anthology, titled *Dreams In Hiding*. Her poetry and short story collections can be found on Amazon.

Learn more:
dreamsinhiding.wixsite.com/mysite

Connect on Social Media:
@dreamsinhiding.writing

About The Publisher

INDIE EARTH

PUBLISHING

Indie Earth Publishing is an independent, author-first co-publishing press based in Miami, FL, dedicated to giving writers the creative freedom they deserve when publishing their poetry, fiction, and short story collections.

Indie Earth provides its authors a plethora of services meant to aid them in their book publishing experiences and finally feel they are releasing the book of their dreams.

With Indie Earth Publishing, you are more than just another author. You are part of the Indie Earth creative family, making a difference one book at a time.

www.indieearthbooks.com

For inquiries, please email:
indieearthpublishinghouse@gmail.com

Instagram: @indieearthbooks